Resisting the Nazis

CLAIRE THROP

T0052970

heinemann
raintree

© 2016 Heinemann-Raintree
an imprint of Capstone Global Library, LLC
Chicago, Illinois

To contact Capstone Global Library please call 800-747-4992, or visit our web site
www.capstonepub.com

Edited by Helen Cox Cannons
Designed by Philippa Jenkins
Original illustrations © Capstone Global Library Limited 2015
Illustrated by HL Studios, Witney, Oxon, England
Picture research by Jo Miller
Production by Helen McCreath
Originated by Capstone Global Library Ltd

Library of Congress Cataloging-in-Publication Data
Throp, Claire.
  Resisting the Nazis / Claire Throp.
     pages cm. — (Heroes of World War II)
  Includes bibliographical references and index.
  ISBN 978-1-4109-8045-8 (hb) — ISBN 978-1-4109-8050-2 (pb) — ISBN 978-1-4109-8060-1 (ebook) 1.
Anti-Nazi movement — History — 20th century — Juvenile literature. 2. Anti-Nazi movement — Europe — Biography —
Juvenile literature. 3. Holocaust, Jewish (1939-1945) — Juvenile literature. 4. Germany — History — 1933-1945 —
Juvenile literature. I. Title.

  DD256.3.T475 2015
  943.086092'2 — dc23   2014044857

This book has been officially leveled by using the F&P Text Level Gradient™ Leveling System.

Acknowledgments
We would like to thank the following for permission to reproduce photographs: Alamy: Everett Collection
Historical, 30, 35, Israel images/Israel Talby, 31, Pictorial Press Ltd, 19; Australian War Memorial, 18; Corbis,
36, Dave G. Houser, 41, Hulton-Deutsch Collection, 32, Ira Nowinski, 17; Dreamstime: Aubrey Thompson, 37;
Gamma-Keystone via Getty Images/Keystone-France, 23, 33; Gamma-Rapho via Getty Images/Daniel Simon,
22; Getty Images: Apic, cover (right), 24, Central Press, 16, Francis Reiss/Haywood Magee, 9, Keystone,
cover (left), Popperfoto, 20, The LIFE Images Collection/Walter Sanders, 27; Glow Images: Heritage Images/
Ann Ronan Pictures, 6, Heritage Images/Fine Arts Images, 39; Landov: Heinrich Hoffman Collection, cover
(background); National Archives and Records Administration, 7, 10; Newscom: dpa/picture-alliance, 8, dpa/
picture-alliance/ADN, 28, Everett Collection, 12, 14, World History Archive, 34, ZB/Archiv/picture alliance/
Berliner Verlag, 11, ZUMA Press/Action Press, 21; Shutterstock: KUCO, 1, pedrosala, 25; SuperStock: age
fotostock/David Cole, 26; The Image Works, 13, akg-images/Wittenstein, 29.

The heroes featured on the front cover are Violette Szabo (left) and Raymond Aubrac (right).

We would like to thank Nick Hunter for his invaluable help in the preparation of this book.

Every effort has been made to contact copyright holders of material reproduced in this book. Any omissions will
be rectified in subsequent printings if notice is given to the publisher.

All the Internet addresses (URLs) given in this book were valid at the time of going to press. However, due to
the dynamic nature of the Internet, some addresses may have changed, or sites may have changed or ceased
to exist since publication. While the author and publisher regret any inconvenience this may cause readers, no
responsibility for any such changes can be accepted by either the author or the publisher.

Printed and bound in the United States of America.
010562RP

Contents

The Story of World War II

World War II began in 1939 and ended in 1945. At first, many people thought that the war would last about six weeks. In fact, it was six long years. During this dark time, many brave people fought to resist Hitler's Nazis.

HOW DID THE WAR START?

On March 12, 1938, Germany invaded its neighboring country, Austria. Germany's leader was Adolf Hitler, head of the National Socialist Party. Members of this political party were known as Nazis. When Hitler pushed the German troops into Czechoslovakia, a deal was signed that stopped Germany from invading other countries, but allowed Germany to keep part of Czechoslovakia. This was called appeasement. However, on September 1, 1939, Germany invaded Poland. Two days later, Great Britain declared war on Germany.

AXIS POWERS VERSUS THE ALLIES

The Axis Powers included Germany, Italy (for part of the war), and Japan. These countries fought against the Allies, which included Britain, France, the Soviet Union (from June 1941), and, from December 1941, the United States.

This map shows how much of Europe and the USSR was occupied by the Axis Powers by 1941. The map also shows the cities that were badly damaged by bombing raids.

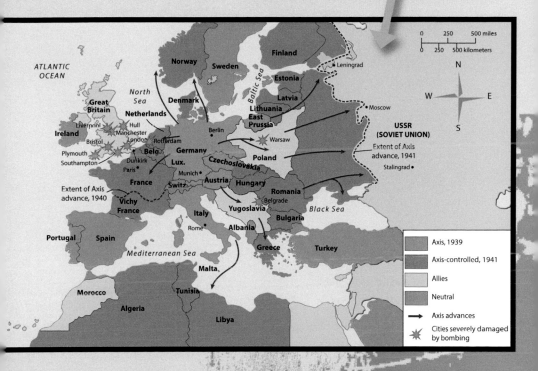

0   250   500 miles
0   250   500 kilometers

N
W   E
S

ATLANTIC
OCEAN

Finland
Leningrad

Norway
Sweden
Estonia
Latvia
Lithuania
East Prussia

North
Sea

Great
Britain

Denmark

Netherlands

Moscow

Liverpool   Hull
Ireland   Manchester
Bristol   London   Rotterdam
Plymouth   Dunkirk   Belg.   Germany
Southampton   Paris   Lux.
France   Switz.

Berlin
Warsaw
Poland

USSR
(SOVIET UNION)

Extent of Axis
advance, 1941

Stalingrad

Czechoslovakia
Munich
Austria   Hungary
Romania
Belgrade
Yugoslavia   Black Sea

Extent of Axis
advance, 1940

Vichy
France

Italy
Rome   Albania   Bulgaria

Portugal   Spain

Mediterranean Sea

Greece   Turkey

Malta

Morocco   Tunisia

Algeria   Libya

Baltic Sea

![]	Axis, 1939
![]	Axis-controlled, 1941
![]	Allies
![]	Neutral
→	Axis advances
✹	Cities severely damaged by bombing

BLITZKRIEG ACROSS EUROPE

By June 1940, German forces had swept across Europe. Denmark, Norway, the Netherlands, Belgium, and most of France had all been invaded. Hitler allowed the French to rule southern France from the town of Vichy, as long as they followed his orders. The German *Blitzkrieg*, or lightning war, used tanks and aircraft to overwhelm opponents. Germany now looked toward Britain. Heroic resistance by the Royal Air Force (RAF) held off the German *Luftwaffe* (air force). On September 17, Hitler abandoned his plans to invade Britain.

British planes fought relentlessly during the Battle of Britain.

THE SPECIAL OPERATIONS EXECUTIVE

During the Battle of Britain, which took place in the summer of 1940, the Special Operations Executive (SOE) was set up by Britain's new prime minister, Winston Churchill. It would link up with resistance movements in Europe and weaken the Nazis in the occupied countries. The first SOE agents were dropped by parachute into France in the spring of 1941.

Japan's attack on Pearl Harbor shocked the United States.

MORE COUNTRIES JOIN THE WAR

In 1941, much of Eastern Europe, from the Baltic Sea to the Balkan Mountains in the south, was already controlled by Germany or friendly governments. On June 22, Germany invaded the Soviet Union during Operation Barbarossa. The Nazis got close to the Soviet capital, Moscow. However, freezing temperatures, terrain made soggy by winter rain, and a ferocious defense proved too much for Nazi soldiers not properly prepared for the cold.

On December 7, Japanese airplanes attacked the U.S. naval base at Pearl Harbor, Hawaii, killing thousands of Americans and destroying more than 20 ships and nearly 200 aircraft. The United States entered the war one day later.

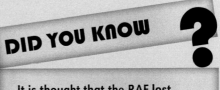

DID YOU KNOW ?

It is thought that the RAF lost 1,023 planes during the Battle of Britain. The Luftwaffe lost 1,887.

LIFE IN OCCUPIED EUROPE

People living under Nazi occupation lost their freedom. Newspapers and media were tightly controlled. Food rations were scarce, and the occupied people were forced to work for the Nazis. Anyone who tried to oppose the invaders risked being arrested, tortured, or executed. Jews faced extreme persecution and, by 1945, around 6 million Jews had been murdered in the Holocaust.

WARSAW GHETTO UPRISING

The Nazis forced Jews to live in particular areas, called ghettos, until they could be executed. The largest was the Warsaw Ghetto, in Poland, which held about 500,000 Jews.

From July 1942, the Nazis sent about 5,000 Jews a day from the ghetto to Treblinka, an extermination (death) camp. Finally, in January 1943, a group called the Jewish Fighting Organization (ZOB) decided to fight back. Then, on April 19, the largest revolt against the Nazis—the Warsaw Ghetto Uprising—began. The resistance fought against 2,000 Nazi troops until, on May 8, ZOB's main bunker was destroyed, leading many to surrender and others to take their own lives.

D-DAY

On June 6, 1944, the Allies crossed from Britain to land on the beaches of Normandy, France. This was D-Day—the start of a major attack on Nazi-occupied Europe. The Allies slowly progressed until the Nazis who were stationed in France's capital, Paris, surrendered on August 25, 1944.

VICTORY AT LAST!

The war in Europe eventually ended on May 8, 1945.
VE (Victory in Europe) Day parties took place all over Europe.

The dropping of atomic bombs on the Japanese cities of Hiroshima and Nagasaki in August forced Japan to surrender. VJ (Victory over Japan) Day was celebrated on August 15, 1945.

Allied countries celebrated the end of the war on VE Day.

What the Resistance Movement Did

The resistance movement was made up of people who were willing to risk their lives helping the Allies to defeat the Nazis in whatever way they could. They carried out a number of different activities:

- They gathered intelligence about the enemy. This included information about the movements of enemy troops.
- They carried out guerrilla warfare.
- They destroyed lines of communication, including railroad lines, and stopped production at factories. These activities are called sabotage.
- They assisted people who had escaped the enemy—for example, pilots whose planes had crashed.
- They openly attacked the Nazis once the Nazi retreat had started.

French resistance fighters always had to be ready to fight.

German soldiers marched into Russia during Operation Barbarossa in 1941.

Resistance movements existed in all German-occupied countries. At first, these movements did not have much impact—there were too many separate groups, all with different ideas. However, the German attack on the Soviet Union in June 1941 changed things. Communist groups throughout Europe now got involved. Many people joined the communist resistance movement because it was seen as the most successful.

By the end of 1941, the SOE found that organizing the different resistance movements across Europe was working. SOE agents were sent to France and other European countries to coordinate the plans and attacks in order to maximize damage to the Nazis.

COMMUNISM

Communism is a type of government and a way of thinking. In a communist state, a country's property is publicly and not privately owned. Wealth is shared among the country's people equally or according to each person's needs. The Soviet Union was a communist country during World War II. This meant that the government owned or was in control of food production, transportation, and land.

SOE recruits were taught how to recognize a German plane.

SOE RECRUITMENT

Men were recruited to the SOE from colleges and top business jobs. From 1942, women were also recruited, but from more varied backgrounds—before World War II, few women went to college or were able to get top jobs. While not everyone agreed with women getting involved in the SOE, many thought that the enemy would take less notice of women when they went undercover.

TRAINING

SOE recruits usually trained for four to nine months, depending on the type of work they would be doing. In Britain, the training often took place in large, historic homes in the country, which the armed forces used for various purposes during the war.

DID YOU KNOW ?

Recruits from outside France were "Frenchified"—they had to do everything in a French way so as not to stand out from real French people when they landed in France, from brushing their hair to placing their silverware after eating. Some even had tooth fillings replaced with French-style gold fillings!

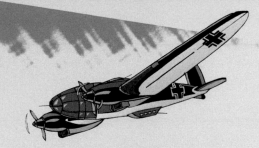

SOE training involved:

- improving physical fitness
- learning how to live off the land, if necessary
- learning how to clean, load, and use guns—including guns from all different countries
- parachute training
- recognizing the ranks of German soldiers and types of plane from their silhouettes in the sky
- recognizing the ranks of French police
- making explosives in order to blow up railroad lines and power stations
- guerrilla warfare
- what to look for when recruiting new resistance fighters
- dealing with interrogation.

SOE agents carried small shovels when they parachuted. This was to help them bury their parachutes after they had landed.

The Resistance Movement in France

Most SOE agents were sent to France. This was because, at first, the Vichy government was running southern France, so there were not as many Nazis in the country. However, it meant that southern France was less eager to join the resistance. It was only when Germany took over the government of all of France, from November 1942, that things changed.

Nazi soldiers and tanks were commonplace in some areas of France by mid-1940.

The agents who went to France worked for F section, an SOE department led by Maurice Buckmaster. F section supplied weapons and trained agents, while the French resistance movement provided intelligence. There were other French resistance groups that the SOE did not control—for example, the communist resistance fighters. On June 22, 1941, all the communist resistance groups joined together, which made them stronger.

There were many brave volunteers who worked for the SOE during the war. The following pages tell the stories of just a few.

THE GESTAPO

The Gestapo was a German secret police force, created to seek out anyone considered a threat to the Nazis. They targeted mainly Jews and resistance fighters. The Gestapo made sure that resistance leaders were publicly executed, as a warning to others. For example, in April 1944, the Nazis put up 15,000 copies of the "Red Poster" in Paris, which showed the faces of 10 of the 23 resistance fighters they had killed in February 1944.

DID YOU KNOW ?

During April and May 1944, the French resistance movement destroyed 1,800 railroad engines. Allied bombers destroyed 2,400 more, making it very difficult for the Nazis to move soldiers and equipment around.

This map shows the main towns and cities in France.

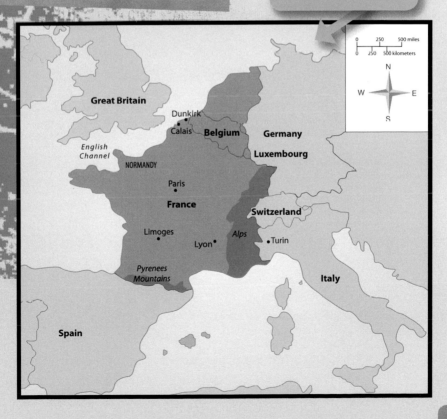

Forest Frederic Edward Yeo-Thomas

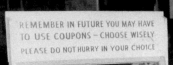

All SOE agents were given code names to help keep their identities secret. Yeo-Thomas was code-named Shelley, Seahorse, and the White Rabbit.

REMEMBER IN FUTURE YOU MAY HAVE TO USE COUPONS – CHOOSE WISELY PLEASE DO NOT HURRY IN YOUR CHOICE

Forest Frederic Edward Yeo-Thomas (1902–64) was born to an English family that had lived in France for over 35 years. He was educated in both England and France. He fought at the end of World War I and for Poland against Russia in 1919–20. He was captured, but the night before he was due to be shot, he escaped. Yeo-Thomas joined the SOE in February 1942.

In 1943, Yeo-Thomas was given the task of finding out what supplies and weapons the Maquis (see page 17) needed. He complained to Winston Churchill about their lack of weapons.

THE MAQUIS

The Maquis were French resistance fighters who used guerrilla warfare to fight against the Nazis. They mainly worked from the mountains of southern France.

CLOSE ESCAPES

Yeo-Thomas was nearly captured six times, but he always managed to remain free. He was finally seized by the Gestapo in March 1944. He was interrogated, tortured, and beaten for four days. He tried to escape twice, but failed. He was kept in Fresnes prison, away from other prisoners, for four months. Given barely any food some weeks, he still refused to give up any information.

He was moved several times to different prisons and concentration camps. During one of these trips, in April 1945, he managed to escape from a train. He finally made it to the Allies' lines and to safety.

Buchenwald concentration camp was one of the largest in Germany. Guard towers and barbed-wire fences were used to prevent the prisoners from escaping.

Nancy Wake

N ancy Wake (1912–2011) was born in Wellington, New Zealand. In the early 1930s, she became a journalist. After seeing the treatment of Jews in Berlin, where she was supposed to be interviewing Hitler, she was filled with anti-Nazi feelings. Wake lived in the south of France and got to know the French way of life. She married a French industrialist in November 1939.

GETTING INVOLVED

Wake began to help prisoners of war and other people escape from France. She also acted as a courier. carrying messages and radio transmitters to other towns. She was twice captured and questioned. only to be released as unimportant. Eventually. however. the Gestapo got too close to the woman they knew as "White Mouse" and she had to use an escape route through the mountains to Spain and then on to Britain.

WORKING FOR THE SOE

In Britain. Wake was accepted into the SOE's F section. She led the French resistance movement. the Maquis. and helped build them into a force of 7.500 resistance fighters. Wake not only made sure that supplies and weapons were provided to the resistance. but she was also often directly involved in guerrilla raids herself. Once. she only narrowly escaped being blown up by a bomb that the Nazis hurled at her van.

This Maquis resistance group is being instructed about a mission.

Violette Szabo

Violette is seen here with her husband in 1940.

Violette Bushell (1921–45) was born in Paris, France, to an English father and French mother. In 1932, the family moved to London. In July 1940, Violette met and married a Hungarian soldier, Captain Étienne Szabo. He was killed in battle in North Africa in 1942.

In July 1943, Szabo joined the SOE, but she didn't impress her trainers. However, her unsatisfactory reports were overruled and, in April 1944, she was sent to France to act as a courier to Philippe Liewer. He was trying to figure out if his resistance network—called Salesman—could be saved after the Nazis had arrested many of its fighters. Szabo returned safely to Britain.

Szabo became the first woman to be awarded the George Cross, a British medal for bravery.

Szabo's second mission to France took place in June 1944. She spent one and a half days cycling around. passing on Liewer's instructions and explosives to supporters.

CAPTURE

While traveling with Dufour. a Maquis leader. Szabo ran into a roadblock. A gunfight took place. but the heavily armed Nazis pushed the two resistance fighters back. Szabo hurt her ankle and told Dufour to leave her. When she ran out of bullets. she was captured.

Szabo was interrogated at the Nazi headquarters at Limoges. but she didn't give up any information. She was moved to Paris and tortured. but still refused to talk. In August. Szabo was taken to Ravensbrück concentration camp and then on to other camps to do hard labor. She returned to Ravensbrück and. on January 27. 1945. was shot.

Szabo showed great courage in refusing to reveal information that would have harmed the resistance. but might have saved her life. She was just 23 years old.

Ravensbrück concentration camp was the only women's concentration camp. This wooden rack was used for beatings.

Raymond Aubrac

Together, Raymond and Lucie were known as "Aubrac."

Raymond Aubrac (1914–2012) was born to Jewish shopkeepers in Vesoul, France. He became a French resistance leader, along with his wife, Lucie. Together, they were involved in creating one of the eight movements that made up the National Resistance Council in France. Raymond also published a secret newspaper called *Libération* (Freedom).

CAPTURE AND RESCUE

Raymond Aubrac and Jean Moulin, another resistance hero, were captured in June 1943 and tortured by Klaus Barbie, head of the Gestapo in Lyon. Moulin died, but Aubrac escaped on October 21, when Lucie led a raid to rescue him. She told the German commander she was pregnant but not married to Aubrac, and persuaded him to agree to let her marry Aubrac before he was executed. When the Nazis were driving him from the wedding ceremony back to Montluc jail, a resistance car overtook the truck and shot the German driver. Raymond escaped, and the Aubracs were flown to London a few months later.

Klaus Barbie was known as the "Butcher of Lyon" as a result of all the people he tortured. He was thought to have been responsible for the deaths of 4,000 people.

SECRET COMMUNICATION

Resistance members had to be careful when carrying out communications. One way of communicating secretly involved leaving certain items on a clothes line. The initial letter of each item would spell out a word—for example, "HELP" (handkerchief, eiderdown [a quilt], lace, pants).

23

Virginia Hall

Virginia Hall (1906–82) was born in Baltimore, Maryland, to a wealthy family. She was educated in Europe. Hall wanted to join the U.S. foreign service but was rejected, partly because she had an artificial leg as a result of a hunting accident years before. So, she moved to London and became a member of the SOE.

DID YOU KNOW?

Hall called her artificial leg Cuthbert!

IN FRANCE

Hall was now a journalist for the *New York Post* newspaper. and under this secret cover. she was sent into Lyon. France. in August 1941. She organized the Heckler network and worked as a courier. She advised new agents. helped people get to escape routes. and recruited new resistance fighters.

When she heard that the Nazis were heading for Lyon in November 1942. she escaped on foot across the Pyrenees Mountains. It took her just 48 hours— in the winter and with an artificial leg! On the Spanish border. she was arrested and imprisoned. but she was saved by the U.S. ambassador.

JOINING THE U.S. OFFICE OF STRATEGIC SERVICES

Hall trained in London as a wireless operator. but she then joined the newly formed U.S. Office of Strategic Services (OSS). Despite being well known by the Gestapo. she volunteered to return to France to set up a new OSS network. She disguised herself as an old woman and organized parachute drops of supplies for resistance groups. in addition to sabotaging bridges and railroad lines.

Walking in the Pyrenees was dangerous at any time, particularly in the winter.

Resistance Movements in Germany

Heinrich Himmler was in charge of getting rid of all the Jews in what was called the "Final Solution."

Other resistance movements existed in Germany, too.

THE EDELWEISS PIRATES

The Edelweiss Pirates was a collection of youth movements. The members hated the way Hitler Youth had taken over the lives of young people in Germany. Hitler Youth was an organization that taught Nazi ideals to young Germans and prepared boys for the military and girls for motherhood.

Heinrich Himmler wanted all Germans—including young people—to be obedient. He demanded that members of youth groups who were disloyal to the Nazis should be sent to concentration camps for two to three years. In November 1944, 13 youths were hanged in Cologne after one of them killed a Nazi informer—6 of them were, or had been, Edelweiss Pirates.

THE CONFESSING CHURCH

The Confessing Church was a group of Christians who were unhappy with Nazi attempts to keep the church under Nazi rule. Some members, such as Dietrich Bonhoeffer, also disagreed with the harsh treatment of Jews and other minority groups.

Bonhoeffer took a job in the Office of Military Intelligence, supposedly in order to promote Nazism. However, he actually used the opportunity to travel to Italy, Switzerland, and Scandinavia to encourage anti-Nazism resistance. He tried—unsuccessfully—to pass information about the resistance movement to Britain in 1942. Bonhoeffer was even involved in attempts on Hitler's life. He was eventually arrested in April 1943 for trying to help Jews escape to neutral Switzerland. He was taken to Buchenwald concentration camp and hanged in April 1945.

Dietrich Bonhoeffer wrote many letters about religion while in prison. After his death, they were published as a book called Letters and Papers from Prison.

Sophie Scholl

Sophie was just 21 years old when the Nazis killed her.

The White Rose movement was focused on peaceful resistance and lasted from June 1942 to February 1943. Students from the University of Munich formed the main body of the group.

The most famous members of the White Rose were Sophie Scholl (1921–43) and her brother, Hans. Their father had already been imprisoned for criticizing Hitler. Sophie and Hans kept the White Rose movement small because it was believed that informants— people who reported suspicious actions to the Nazi secret police, the Gestapo— were everywhere.

DID YOU KNOW ?

In the fall of 1943, a copy of the White Rose's last leaflet was smuggled to the Allies. It was copied and dropped all over Germany.

LEAFLETS AND GRAFFITI

Only six leaflets were ever produced, and members secretly distributed the anti-war, anti-Nazi leaflets to random addresses in Munich. There was also a graffiti campaign. Resistance fighters sprayed "Down with Hitler" onto walls in Munich.

On February 18, 1943, Hans and Sophie decided to leave copies of their sixth leaflet where students at the University of Munich would see them after their classes. When Sophie threw some leaflets over a balcony, she was seen by the university janitor. He reported it to the Gestapo.

EXECUTION

Sophie, Hans, and their friend Christoph Probst were arrested. All three were executed on February 22, 1943, in Munich. Another White Rose member, Alexander Schmorell, tried to escape but was also later executed.

"What does my death matter, if through us thousands of people are awakened and stirred to action?"

Sophie Scholl

Sophie is seen here with her brother, Hans (left), and Christoph Probst (right).

Resistance in Other Countries

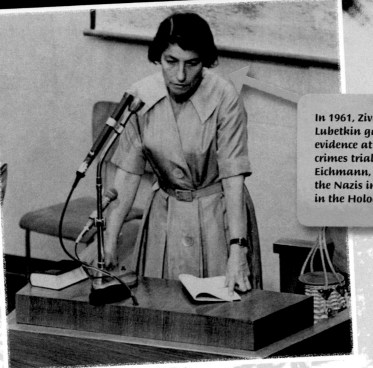

In 1961, Zivia Lubetkin gave evidence at the war crimes trial of Adolf Eichmann, one of the Nazis involved in the Holocaust.

Resistance movements existed in other countries, too. Many were linked to the SOE or the OSS in Germany.

ZIVIA LUBETKIN

Zivia Lubetkin (1914–76) was a founder of ZOB and its only female leader. The day before the Nazis discovered the bunker in which the leaders were hiding during the Warsaw Ghetto Uprising on May 8, 1943, Lubetkin was sent to find an escape route through the sewers. She was one of only 34 ZOB resistance fighters to survive the war.

Lubetkin's first name in Polish—Cywia—became code for "Poland" in many resistance communications. She went on to take part in the Polish Warsaw Uprising in 1944, when the Polish resistance tried to free Warsaw from Nazi occupation. After the war, she helped thousands of Jews to leave Poland.

MORDECHAI ANIELEWICZ

Mordechai Anielewicz (1919–43) was in western Poland when thousands of Jews in the Warsaw Ghetto were executed during the summer of 1942. He went to Warsaw and persuaded the Jewish leaders to resist the Nazis. The ZOB was founded as a result. Anielewicz became the ghetto's leader after surviving a clash with the Nazis in January 1943. Two thousand troops returned to the ghetto on April 19 (see page 8). When they gassed the bunker where ZOB's leaders were hiding, many people surrendered, but Anielewicz and others took their own lives rather than be sent to Treblinka.

THE HOLOCAUST

The Nazis wanted to wipe out the Jews. They destroyed Jewish businesses and places of worship and forced many Jews to live in ghettos or sent them to concentration camps. The Nazis also persecuted other groups, such as the Roma (sometimes known as gypsies) and homosexuals. Between 1933 and 1945, 6 million Jews were murdered, many in extermination camps that were built specifically to kill them.

This is a statue of Mordechai Anielewicz, in Israel.

ITALY

Italy had a number of resistance fighters who provided fast intelligence and impressive sabotage skills. They were successful partly because the SOE and OSS provided them with weapons and supplies. They used an OSS radio to communicate with the Fifteenth Army Group, the Allied army based in Italy.

ENNIO TASSINARI

OSS agent Ennio Tassinari heard that partisans had managed to get hold of Nazi military plans. These plans showed a weak spot in the Gothic Line, which was the Nazi line of defense north of Florence, Italy. The Gothic Line blocked the route to Austria. Tassinari smuggled a copy of the plans in the soles of his shoes from Lucca to Siena, Italy, a distance of over 87 miles (140 kilometers). This helped the Allies to break through the line in the fall of 1944.

Breaking through the Gothic Line in Italy proved important for the Allied war effort.

Italian resistance fighters, like these at a parade marking the freeing of Milan in 1945, worked hard for the Allies.

RICCARDO VANZETTI

Riccardo Vanzetti was one of three men dropped into the Alps near the French border in March 1944. The group's leader, Marcello de Leva, set about creating a new intelligence network in Turin. Vanzetti remained in the country and trained saboteurs to disturb German communication lines. He also developed a system of mobile partisan attacks, first using bicycles, then cars and trucks—all of which were stolen from the enemy.

DID YOU KNOW?

Vanzetti made sure that the Nazis wouldn't discover his team's radio by hiding it in a beehive! The radio operator was able to communicate throughout the war—even when Nazis were in the same farmhouse the team was living in!

CZECHOSLOVAKIA

In early 1940, the Central Leadership of Resistance at Home (UVOD) was created to join together all Czechoslovakian resistance movements. The communist groups joined after Operation Barbarossa (see page 7).

REINHARD HEYDRICH

In September 1941, Reinhard Heydrich—a high-ranking Nazi official—was sent to Prague to deal with anti-Nazi feeling in Czechoslovakia. About 5,000 people thought to be part of the resistance movement were imprisoned. This action only encouraged UVOD to sabotage more Nazi operations.

Then, on May 27, 1942, Czech agents trained by the SOE parachuted in from Britain and bombed Heydrich's car. He was seriously wounded and died on June 4.

Heydrich was known as "The Hangman."

Nazi soldiers can be seen here looking at the bodies of the men of Lidice.

REVENGE

UVOD had not agreed with the plan to kill Heydrich because they feared what the Nazis might do in revenge. They were right to be scared. Hitler was furious and ordered the destruction of the village of Lidice near Prague, in Czechoslovakia. The men were shot, and the women were taken to Ravensbrück concentration camp, where most were killed. Most of the children were given to other families and raised as Germans. Lidice was then burned and flattened, as though it had never existed.

CHANGE OF PLAN

After this tragedy, the Czech government advised UVOD to stop using sabotage and stick to gaining intelligence for the SOE instead. UVOD was particularly successful at gathering intelligence from as far away as the Balkans.

The communist resistance worked with Soviet resistance fighters and gradually persuaded more people to join them. Eventually, the cooperation that had existed between the communist resistance and UVOD was lost.

NORWAY

The Norwegian Secret Army was known as Milorg (which stood for "military organization"). It was particularly successful at sabotaging factories. It was well equipped by SOE because the long Norwegian coastline and border with neutral Sweden made supply drops easier.

The Vemork power plant at Rjukan was producing heavy water to make plutonium for the Nazis. This was needed in order to carry out atomic bomb research. The plant was sabotaged by 12 Norwegian commandos, but their attack was based on intelligence that Milorg had provided. The men lived in the mountains and then crossed a river at the bottom of a gorge to reach the power plant. They then had to get inside the building, overpower the German guards, and set explosives. Amazingly, they were successful. After the Nazis got the power plant running again six months later, it was bombed by U.S. aircraft.

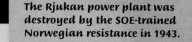

The Rjukan power plant was destroyed by the SOE-trained Norwegian resistance in 1943.

GUNNAR SØNSTEBY

Gunnar Sønsteby (1918–2012) wrote a book called *Report from No. 24*— he was SOE agent number 24. Sønsteby volunteered for Milorg, but he decided to speed things up by offering to help the pro-Nazi Norwegian police. He made a number of trips to Sweden in order to report intelligence to the SOE. He also learned how to forge German documents, and his disguises allowed him freedom of travel. He even smuggled printing plates to produce Norwegian paper money in Sweden, which helped to pay for the SOE's activities in Norway.

The Shetland Bus service (actually boats) was famed for smuggling agents as well as supplies across the North Sea. Norwegian Leif Larsen made 52 trips and even became known as "Shetland's Larsen"! This is the memorial to the Shetland Bus.

THE SOVIET UNION

The resistance fighters in the Soviet Union were known as partisans. Most partisans were based in the Pripet Marshes, wet areas of land southwest of the capital, Moscow. The Belorussian forests were also important for the partisans. They knew the land in both these areas better than the Germans, which made it easy for them to attack the Nazis, but difficult for the Nazis to fight back. Instead, the Nazis attacked ordinary people because they could not find or capture the partisans. However, this just caused more people to join the partisans.

"They would attack us unexpectedly, as if rising from under the earth. They cut us up to disappear like devils..."

Friedrich Buschele, a German who was killed by Belorussians

This map shows the location of the Pripet Marshes. At this time, Ukraine, Belorussia, and Russia were all part of the Soviet Union.

In May 1942, the Central Staff was set up to organize the partisans. By July 1943, it is thought that there were about 142,000 partisans in the Soviet Union. The Soviet Union's leader, Joseph Stalin, made sure that the partisans, particularly larger groups such as the Kovpak brigade, were well equipped to be successful against the Nazis. Damage to German property, supply lines, and communications played a huge part in limiting the Nazis' success in Russia.

Sydir Kovpak was a Soviet hero.

SYDIR KOVPAK

Sydir Kovpak (1887–1967) was the leader of a Ukrainian partisan force that fought against the Nazis—the Ukrainian Insurgent Army. It used guerrilla warfare tactics to attack the Nazis as far away as the border with Romania. Kovpak was awarded the title Hero of the Soviet Union twice—in 1942 and 1944. It was an award given for a heroic act.

Map showing Europe in 1945:

- 0 250 500 miles
- 0 250 500 kilometers
- N / W / E / S

Karelia
Finland
Norway
Sweden
North Sea
Baltic Sea
Estonia
Soviet Union
Denmark
Latvia
East Prussia
Polish Control
Lithuania
Polish Control
Netherlands
Great Britain
BRITISH ZONE
Berlin
SOVIET ZONE
Poland
Byelorussia (Belarus)
Belgium
Germany
Czechoslovakia
Luxembourg
FRENCH ZONE
U.S. ZONE
Ruthenia
Bessarabia
Switzerland
Austria
Hungary
France
Slovenia
Romania
Black Sea
Italy
Yugoslavia
Spain
Mediterranean Sea
Albania
Bulgaria
Greece
Turkey

World War II would not have been won by the Allies without the brave people who were dropped into enemy territory in order to organize and assist the resistance movement. Some of their acts of sabotage were essential to the war effort. What if the Nazis had been able to continue production of heavy water at the Vemork power plant, and use it to produce atomic bombs? The war may have ended differently.

This map shows Europe in 1945, when the war ended. Germany was divided, and its capital city, Berlin, was under Allied control. Today, Europe is very different.

PROBLEMS

However, the resistance movement was not successful in all countries. In the Netherlands, for example, an agent was captured and forced to keep sending messages to the SOE. Despite the fact that the agent sent codes arranged beforehand to tell the SOE he'd been caught, more agents were sent to rescue him, and they, too, were captured.

Many people, including some who worked there, viewed the SOE as disorganized and believed that resistance work caused more problems than it solved. The governments of some occupied countries worried that it might result in civil war when World War II was over, but SOE agents continued to work tirelessly to try to make a difference.

A LOVE OF COUNTRY

The men and women who were chosen to be SOE agents were smart, brave, good with languages, and able to blend in with local people. Along with local resistance fighters, they put a love of country and a wish to help end the war above their own safety. U.S. Allied Supreme Commander Dwight D. Eisenhower thought the work of the French resistance movement was equal to that of six divisions of soldiers. This alone shows just how important the resistance was.

This is the monument to the Warsaw Uprising, in front of the Poland Supreme Court in Warsaw.

Timeline

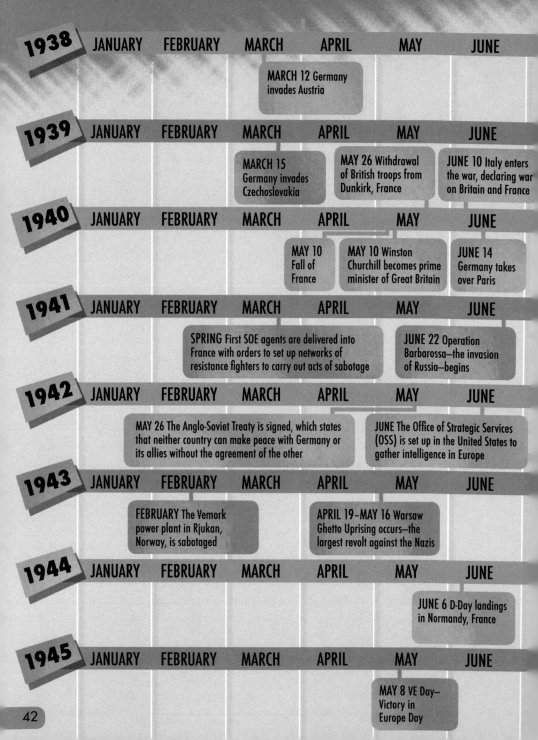

1938   JANUARY   FEBRUARY   MARCH   APRIL   MAY   JUNE

MARCH 12 Germany invades Austria

1939   JANUARY   FEBRUARY   MARCH   APRIL   MAY   JUNE

MARCH 15 Germany invades Czechoslovakia

MAY 26 Withdrawal of British troops from Dunkirk, France

JUNE 10 Italy enters the war, declaring war on Britain and France

1940   JANUARY   FEBRUARY   MARCH   APRIL   MAY   JUNE

MAY 10 Fall of France

MAY 10 Winston Churchill becomes prime minister of Great Britain

JUNE 14 Germany takes over Paris

1941   JANUARY   FEBRUARY   MARCH   APRIL   MAY   JUNE

SPRING First SOE agents are delivered into France with orders to set up networks of resistance fighters to carry out acts of sabotage

JUNE 22 Operation Barbarossa—the invasion of Russia—begins

1942   JANUARY   FEBRUARY   MARCH   APRIL   MAY   JUNE

MAY 26 The Anglo-Soviet Treaty is signed, which states that neither country can make peace with Germany or its allies without the agreement of the other

JUNE The Office of Strategic Services (OSS) is set up in the United States to gather intelligence in Europe

1943   JANUARY   FEBRUARY   MARCH   APRIL   MAY   JUNE

FEBRUARY The Vemork power plant in Rjukan, Norway, is sabotaged

APRIL 19–MAY 16 Warsaw Ghetto Uprising occurs—the largest revolt against the Nazis

1944   JANUARY   FEBRUARY   MARCH   APRIL   MAY   JUNE

JUNE 6 D-Day landings in Normandy, France

1945   JANUARY   FEBRUARY   MARCH   APRIL   MAY   JUNE

MAY 8 VE Day— Victory in Europe Day

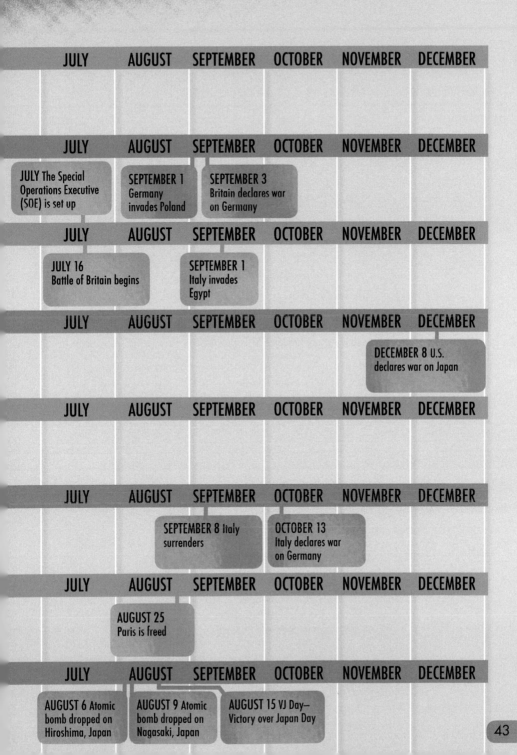

JULY	AUGUST	SEPTEMBER	OCTOBER	NOVEMBER	DECEMBER

JULY	AUGUST	SEPTEMBER	OCTOBER	NOVEMBER	DECEMBER

JULY The Special Operations Executive (SOE) is set up

SEPTEMBER 1 Germany invades Poland

SEPTEMBER 3 Britain declares war on Germany

JULY	AUGUST	SEPTEMBER	OCTOBER	NOVEMBER	DECEMBER

JULY 16 Battle of Britain begins

SEPTEMBER 1 Italy invades Egypt

JULY	AUGUST	SEPTEMBER	OCTOBER	NOVEMBER	DECEMBER

DECEMBER 8 U.S. declares war on Japan

JULY	AUGUST	SEPTEMBER	OCTOBER	NOVEMBER	DECEMBER

JULY	AUGUST	SEPTEMBER	OCTOBER	NOVEMBER	DECEMBER

SEPTEMBER 8 Italy surrenders

OCTOBER 13 Italy declares war on Germany

JULY	AUGUST	SEPTEMBER	OCTOBER	NOVEMBER	DECEMBER

AUGUST 25 Paris is freed

JULY	AUGUST	SEPTEMBER	OCTOBER	NOVEMBER	DECEMBER

AUGUST 6 Atomic bomb dropped on Hiroshima, Japan

AUGUST 9 Atomic bomb dropped on Nagasaki, Japan

AUGUST 15 VJ Day— Victory over Japan Day

Glossary

agent person who works, often in secret, to obtain information for a government

Allies countries, such as Great Britain, France, the Soviet Union, and the United States, that fought against the Axis Powers

atomic bomb bomb that produces an extremely powerful explosion when atoms are split apart

Axis Powers countries, including Germany, Italy, and Japan, that were the enemies of the Allies

bunker underground shelter

communism political system in which wealth and land are owned collectively, by everyone, through the government

concentration camp place where many people are imprisoned, often in horrific conditions. The camps were sometimes used to hold people before execution or used as hard labor camps.

courage bravery

courier person who carries messages and information from one agent to another

Gestapo German secret police

guerrilla warfare type of warfare that differs from traditional warfare in that short, sharp attacks are made on the enemy. This type of warfare is often carried out by people who know the area well and are able to escape quickly before the enemy can respond.

industrialist someone who owns or has financial interest in the business of industry, such as manufacturing

intelligence secret information that has political or military value, including coded messages that are figured out

interrogate question a person aggressively

Jew person who believes in a form of religion called Judaism

Nazi member of the National Socialist Party in Germany

network group of people linked by a common aim

neutral not taking a side

occupied country country that is under the control of another. In World War II, Nazi Germany occupied other countries, including Poland.

partisan member of an armed resistance group

prime minister leader of the government in some countries

recruit persuade someone to join a particular group

sabotage deliberately destroy or disrupt something

Soviet Union Union of Soviet Socialist Republics (USSR), the communist country that existed from 1922 until 1991. Present-day Russia was part of the Soviet Union.

surrender give in to a stronger person or force

torture cause people pain to make them give up information

uprising act of fighting back against an enemy

Vichy government government of France after it was defeated by Germany during World War II. It worked with the Nazis, even helping to capture Jews for them.

volunteer do something by choice

wireless operator person who sent messages using a radio

Find Out More

BOOKS

Adams, Simon. *World War II* (DK Eyewitness). New York: Dorling Kindersley, 2014.

Atwood, Kathryn J. *Women Heroes of World War II* (Women of Action). Chicago: Chicago Review Press, 2011.

Burgan, Michael. *World War II Spies: An Interactive History Adventure* (You Choose). Mankato, Minn.: Capstone, 2013.

Perritano, John. *World War II: Ten Greatest Heroes*. New York: Scholastic, 2011.

WEB SITES

www.museumofworldwarii.com/resistance
This web site provides more information about the resistance movement in World War II.

www.nationalww2museum.org/learn/education/for-students/ww2-history
The National World War II Museum's web site has a useful section full of information written for students.

www.pbs.org/thewar
This is a companion web site to a PBS documentary called *The War*, which explored World War II through people's individual memories and stories.

PLACES TO VISIT

National World War II Museum
945 Magazine Street
New Orleans, Louisiana 70130
nationalww2museum.org

United States Holocaust Memorial Museum
100 Raoul Wallenberg Place, SW
Washington, D.C. 20024
www.ushmm.org

FURTHER RESEARCH

- See if you can find out more about some of the other resistance fighters during the war. Pearl Witherington, who was described as "the best shot, male or female, we have yet had," had several narrow escapes. Captain Peter Churchill and Odette Hallowes worked for the resistance in France, and a movie was made in 1950 called *Odette*, which celebrated Odette's life.
- Investigate the relationship between the SOE and the OSS. Did things run smoothly? Was there any mistrust?
- Resistance movements in a number of countries have been mentioned in this book. Research what happened in other places, such as Greece, Belgium, and North Africa.
- You could also try to learn more about World War II in general. You could explore why Britain and France chose to use appeasement rather than go to war in 1938, or the history of what Americans thought about joining the war effort, both before and after the attack on Pearl Harbor.

Index